Louisiana Midrash

University of New Orleans Press
Manufactured in the United States of America
All rights reserved
ISBN: 978-1-60801-168-1

Interior Design: Ann Hackett
Cover Design: Kevin Stone

This project is made possible by the generous support of
the New Orleans Jazz & Heritage Foundation

UNIVERSITY OF NEW ORLEANS PRESS
RUNAGATE PRESS
-Promulgating New Orleans and African-Heritage Cultures-
Kalamu ya Salaam & Oyawande Ekundayo Fayemi Akanbi
(Kysha Brown Robinson)
Founders
unopress.org

Louisiana Midrash

Marian D. Moore

acknowledgements

Thanks to the editors of the following journals where these poems appeared.

Bridges: A Jewish Feminist Journal: "Dry Bones" and "Tamar Writes"
The Louisiana Review: "For My Father," "Swimming Lessons," and "A Trip to the Zoo"
vox poetica (online): "Mixed Multitude"
ReformJudaism.org: "Yehuda"

table of contents

Midrash

Musings

introduction

In *The Good Book: Reading the Bible With Mind and Heart*, the Rev. Peter Gomes, minister at The Memorial Church at Harvard, writes disapprovingly of a popular method of Bible study where the "Bible is simply the entry into a discussion about more interesting things, usually about oneself." In these discussions, Gomes says, every scripture read is followed by, "What does this mean to you?"

"The answers come thick and fast," Gomes writes, "and we are off into the life stories or personal situations of the group." He allows that such conversations might constitute good therapy but writes, "this is not Bible study, and to call it such is to perpetuate a fiction."

But if we are to also read the scriptures with our hearts, as the title of Gomes' book commands, don't we have to ask some form of "What does this mean to me?" or "What does this mean to us?" or "What does this mean this many thousand years later?"

To be sure, in *Louisiana Midrash,* Marian Moore isn't just looking into the scriptures as if into a mirror. Her poems also put these scriptures under a microscope.

Perhaps it's better to make reference here to her computer science training and say that she's testing the scriptures for some kind of logic. Whichever metaphor we use, it's obvious that Moore possesses the kind of inquisitive mind that's also necessary to better understand the Bible.

I was tempted there to cut the adverb and simply refer to what's necessary to understand the Bible. But better understanding it is likely our only hope. Charles A. Tindley, a prominent hymnodist in the Methodist

Church—Moore's church when she was a child—asserts in a famous composition that "We'll Understand It Better By and By."

Yes, Tindley was referring to trouble, but what's the Bible if not a compendium of trouble?

There's Ishmael, whose inconvenient existence leads to his being denied access to his father. And Esau, who must have wondered if cheaters ever lose. There's Tamar. Her father, the giant-slayer, sits on his hands when her brother rapes her and then weeps when that rapist is killed. "He's my son," King David explains in one of Moore's poems, "and you're only my daughter."

In her poem, "Scapegoat," there's even trouble for the animals, even some of those animals that made it through the great flood.

"Our saviors / Sacrificed us in thanks / as they prepared / to people the land / Now miraculously dry."

Some saviors.

Moore's overlapping identities give rise to the tension that is present in her poems. She's Black and Southern and woman and Jewish, with an affinity for science and science fiction. Each one of those identities informs another identity. Take her poem about her family's farmland being stolen, never to be returned: "My Jewish family would call this a pogrom; / my Black one—just business as usual— / Black folk having their land stolen."

But belonging to multiple worlds can mean not fitting neatly inside any one of them. With these poems we see Moore pulling off paradoxes. She's embracing individuality. She's celebrating community. She's steeped in tradition. She's charting new directions.

Her computer science expertise and her love of science fiction might lead some to doubt that she belongs in the world of poetry. But Moore quells those doubts on every page of this debut volume. This book is evidence of a sharp mind and of a capacious heart.

Midrash

My early studies taught me that one of the tenets of the early Protestants was that scripture belonged to the people. They pried the Christian bible away from the priests and church leaders, insisting that anyone could understand its plain meaning. Thereafter, to borrow a quote, "a hundred flowers bloomed" as each sect interpreted scripture to match its belief.

The Hebrew Scriptures have been the property of the Jewish people since the time of early Rabbis at least. There is an old story in which the Rabbis of the Assembly remind a voice from Heaven that the Torah is not in Heavens—a direct quote from Deuteronomy. What Torah means and how Judaism is practiced is defined by Jews. Consequently, if you pick up a Bible in your local synagogue, it will be heavier than the Christian Bible that you'd find in a church—even though the Christian Bible has more books. You will find the text surrounded by commentary informed by thousands of years of study. Some commentary explicates the "plain" meaning of the text. (Hebrew has changed; our society has changed.) Some of the commentaries are laws that seem to directly contradict what is in the original text. (An eye for an eye was never practiced according to the Rabbis.) And some are stories that fill in the gaps. (If you "remember" that Abraham smashed his father's idols, then you've heard midrash because that story is nowhere in the Hebrew Bible.) Midrashim continue to be written. As Ben Bag Bag said in the first century C.E., "Turn it, and turn it, for everything is in it."

Literary Children

And when Rachel saw that she bare Jacob no children, Rachel envied her sister; and said unto Jacob, Give me children, or else I die. Genesis 30:1

Their wedding gift was
Abraham's biography.
When Jacob tells the story,
at its high point,
the old man strides
along the mountain ridge with God
arguing for the souls of Sodom,
for Lot and lost Gomorrah.

Jacob reads the story to Leah's children as they fall
    asleep each night.
Leah's eyes meet Rachel's
not in triumph
but in understanding.
The only letter that Leah writes is
love on the hearts of her children, silent
vowels beneath Jacob's deeper impressions.
The only poem that Rachel can pen is
written in tears as her sons leave her
remains behind.

Typically, Leah and Rachel are seen as competitors. However, Rachel's words are true for both women. They have little control over the official family narrative. Their lives, as we know them, are defined solely by their male children.

Esau's Farewell #1

He likes the robe, I can tell.
That is how I draw him in—
Like a clay pot on a tenuous rope lowered
into one of our grandfather's wells.
My father went from contention

to accord with his neighbors by freeing
three limestone springs.
I must get there with one homespun garment.

It is an awkward dance. He sits;
I serve. I hear
his sons stamping in the afternoon chill—
anxious to be off, to Egypt
where they all expect to be princes.
Their scorned niece is wife
to the brother they sold.
We are family, is not every slight
absolved by time and distance?

As we talk, Jacob's fingers brush the
twisted loops of fine goat hair—
speckled black and silver from his own flock
mingled with the brick red of my own.
I keep him talking as long as I can.
This old man, my twin,
that I will never see again.
I live in a house where my sons mumble
     thanks to the Hittite gods of my wives,
but I am as much Abraham's blood
as this old man. We have much in common.
In the end, I give him the robe.
It rolls up as tight as a memory.
It pleases me to think of it wrapping him in sleep.

It struck me that Esau, because of his choice of brides, is the only Jew in his household. When Joseph asks that his father Jacob join him in Egypt, he separates the twins forever. In the poem, Esau has one last visit with his twin, Jacob. He has one last chance to say farewell to this living reminder of his heritage.

Esau's Farewell #2

I stand
beneath the shade of my tent.
I watch:
the driver is an arrogant figure:
an Egyptian, a man of the upper Nile.
Dark
as the horses
that pull his chariot.
Older
than I expected.
The gold threads that bind
his hair are twisted amidst living silver.
He remains behind the reins.
Pharaoh's slave will
not place a beaded sandal
upon our loamy soil.

The chariot driver bends;
he lifts my brother Jacob.
I see:
the boy that I directed
to the fields of Dothan,
the young man sent down to slavery.
Joseph lays his fingers
across the glad cries of this father.
Officially,
Pharaoh's minister never left Egypt's soil and
never set foot on his native land.

Should I go out? Find
out if Joseph's forgiveness
extends to the stranger that found him
seeking his brothers in the fields of Shechem?
The man who pointed him to Dothan
to the pit, to peonage in Egypt?
I have a plea of my own.
One day, I will say,
Bring Israel back to his land:
the land of his fathers,
and the land of his brother.

Genesis 37:15-17 And a certain man found him, and, behold, he was wandering in the field. And the man asked him, saying: 'What seekest thou?' And he said: 'I seek my brethren. Tell me, I pray thee, where they are feeding the flock.' And the man said: 'They are departed hence; for I heard them say: Let us go to Dothan.' And Joseph went after his brethren, and found them in Dothan.

The Caves of Machpelah

Genesis 25: 8-9
And Abraham breathed his last, dying at a good age, old and contented....His sons Isaac and Ishmael buried him in the caves Machpelah...

Come near dear Issac
as I parse yet another postcard.
Whisper in my ear forefather,
as I have given up on letters.
Through what conduit
Should I appeal:
 "Please call...."
"Please contact..."
The line than joins us is disconnected;
and Ma Bell has no listing.
Your brother Ishmael dwelt in Egypt
but my own is only 548 miles away—
eight hours by car
days by camel.
Could you pick up some ancient horn,
say briefly—
He's dead.
Did you know that Ishmael would fly to comfort
you, as brother?
How to express such mixed emotions?
This is the man who tossed me to the desert winds;
This is the father who raised a knife to my throat;
He's dead.
The only father I ever knew.
The only father I never had.

Mixed Multitude

I am the man who
chasing an errant lamb, glimpses
the flicker of flame but turns aside
to rescue the missing. I return
to my flock, wary
of wolves in this wilderness.

I am the woman who hears
a burning
melody tumbling from russet leaves.
God sings from a cleft in the rock.
Yet, I go back to camp,
remembering my ailing mother
and the water that I carry.

I am the retinue that must be rescued.
By Moses, by Harriet,
by Toussaint in his borrowed uniform.
Released from my servitude; I hold
my head high—brazen
enough to ask for back wages.
Tell the prophet that I was loyal
to family
if not to God.
I preserved the blaze of life
and I know where the bones of my forebears

are buried.

Miriam

Miriam stands on Fannin Street
four blocks from the Red River and
sings Leadbelly for the mixed multitude of Shreveport.

She is close enough to the fire
hydrant on the corner that
no one wonders at the pool
of water welling at her feet.

For the most part
the men ignore her
They step from one glass bank to another
and her sistrums' slim jangle never enters
their ear
drums.

It is the women pausing
to rub their heeled ensconced feet
who hear the tiny ting of finger cymbals.
Between the glass towers, they see
a shimmering figure bidding them to dance.

Traditionally, Miriam is also considered to be a prophet. She prophesies Moses' birth; she is one of the midwives who refuse to kill newborn Israelite boys. She leads the women of Israel in dance after their exodus from Egypt. She is credited with the presence of water during their journey through the wilderness. The verse that follows her death reads "the community was without water."

Aaron Steers

Aaron is a safe driver
except when he crosses a bridge.
His sister is gone,
his brother distant,
But still—
the van drifts into the center
over the double yellow lines
as if Moses were there pulling on his left arm
Miriam, his right.

When they were there,
his own prophetic flame would burn,
rising up fitfully from his gut
with words never spoken.
Now, he clutches the wheel
painfully aware of grumbling children in the back seat
their voices rising over the firing of the engine.
Aaron steers fitfully, fearful of what may be waiting
as the crest of the span approaches.

*By tradition, Aaron is seen as a peacemaker. He would meet sep-
arately with arguing parties until they would agree to face each
other as friends. He delayed the construction of the Golden Calf
and then participated in its assembly just to prevent dissension.
Here, I envisioned him as seeking the middle path—not always
the best choice on a busy throughway.*

Judges

They said "Call Samson here and let him dance for us." Samson was fetched from the prison and he danced for them. They then put him between the pillars.
-Judges 16:25

So, when some tabloid claimed that they spent September
    ten in discos,
whirling around the dance floor with forbidden women.
I could not imagine;
I did not believe.
Until, waking, I saw Samson
Eyes closed, but not blinded
His sandy hair in two long bead-adorned braids.
Azure tie dyed T-shirt reaching down to his knees
Ruby robe below that, down to his bare feet
He traced patterns in the dust
dancing to the music of African revolution.
The surrounding Philistines pointed and laughed;
snapped photos and videos for the friends back home.
So many innocent people!
All that was needed was twin pillars
And the temple could have fallen again.

Jeremiah in Egypt

Amidst the smoke of hanging torches
beyond the murmer of
gossiping crowds, the old blues man sits
down beneath the city gate.

Some ignorant
well-wisher has thrust a small
harp into his hands begging for
a song of descent,
for weary words to dull their
drunken delight.
No matter.
This is a motley mob:
Ebony children of distant Sheba
mingled with the cedar progeny of Pharaoh.
Each with his own proud tomb
glutted with painted images
occupied by burnished lies.
All of their women pale and thin with flowing black
     twists
All of their men red and square shouldered with noble
     brows
And all of their slaves
smiling
as they bend to their work.
Jeremiah tunes his instrument.
He can cover "Lamentations";
smooth progressions of aleph, beth, gimel
flow over his tongue like bitter myrrh.
He can moan "Alas, the forlorn city"
as if the words were his own

Gritting his teeth only at the lines
That praise a blind King
who agreed to toss him into a well.
This throng will like that; their bodies
swaying like waves in easy sympathy.
And this paycheck will easily cover his rent
leaving a shekel or two
for the stone-faced children of Israel

In Ezekiel, God tells the prophet "Indeed, to them you are nothing more than one who sings love songs with a beautiful voice and plays an instrument well...." Suddenly, I no longer saw the soapbox screamers from "Life of Brian". I saw the prophets as more like Sam Cooke singing "A Change Gonna Come" or Richie Havens singing "Fates". Here, I present Jeremiah in exile in Egypt. People still want to hear the old "songs".

Elijah's Lament

The wind will eventually devour me
Wear away my rough edges
Consume my struggle with words
Replace my ambiguity
With angular arguments.
You, who stare aghast
Will wonder what spirit
Has possessed me
Whose breath informs my lungs?
Who fills my eyes with fire?

I am a window
Through which an otherworldly light shines.
One fault and I would crack
Into shining pebbles at your feet.
A bitter flame bleaches my bones
Thins my blood
Burns the back of my eyes
Until I am blind
To all but the penitent heart.

Tamar Writes

Tamar writes to her father David,
King of all Israel.
She is uncertain
if he even knows her name.
Annon is lettered, but Tamar had no tutor.
Raped and disgraced, she
writes in the only language that she knows
after that night—
every bundle of cloth that she weaves
has one broken thread.
When held to light, the linen tunics that she makes
have a tiny tear: a fault in its warp,
too small to call for discard,
too great to wear to her brothers' many weddings.
Every meal that Tamar cooks
is missing one spice.
The royal taster rolls it onto his tongue, and
declares it safe but unfulfilling.
The wine that she pours into the King's bowl
loses its dark flavor;
like water, it is quickly forgotten on the tongue.
That is what it means to be the King's Daughter.
I know this, when
standing in the cold that pours from your eyes.
I am baptized by flames;
I am washed clean of illusions.
"Of course," you say,
"It's your fault. He's my son,
and you're only
my daughter."

Dry Bones

I saw an angel yesterday.

It was the weekend before Mardi Gras and he was masking as the prophet Ezekiel. He was shaking a tambourine over Lafon Street.

The angel was the very image of my grandfather: an old papershell-pecan colored man dancing in pin stripes. One foot glided over shards of glass, and one hand gripped a circlet of stretched goatskin. He brushed those tin rattles against his thigh and raised the ancient noisemaker to the skies. Standing on my cousin's doorstep, he banged and shouted: "Can these bones live?"

And right away, I knew that he meant New Orleans. And instantly, I knew that it wasn't Ezekiel.
Not my grandfather, and not the priest who saw the chariot; not the Jewish prophet and not the Louisiana sharecropper that I never knew. Can these bones live? No, those are God's lines, not Ezekiel's. It was God who cried out "Dare me, will you? Dare me to resurrect these bones!"

"Hineni, Angel," I called, "Here I am and all. But is this the best that you can do? The East needs more than a song and dance man; the Lower Nine earned more than a tambourine. And where you going to get second-liners in this wilderness? The bones, they sent to St. Gabriel. The live ones, they packed off to Houston."

But angels? They are single-minded. That woman-drum, he gave to me and he went stepping on. Now what I'm supposed to do with it, tell me? And who is there to hear me play?

Jonathan's Lad

1

My robe draped about my hips,
I fettle arrowheads.
"You are as golden as ripen wheat,"
Jonathan whispers in my ear.
I am a field of wheat, I reply.
I am a bundle of bound barley.
He has forgotten how I came to be here:
My father's debt,
His doting paternal king,
The deal stuck until jubilee.
I am Jonathan's slave.

2

I am Jonathan's slave.
My master's draw is strong;
His arrows fly true.
On the morning of the new moon, he says
Run, boy
Go farther. Already, I go
further than any man,
further than any slave,
further than his father knows.
When I look back, my arms
full of barbed staves,
I see them embracing:
Jonathan, the king's son,
David, the king's champion.
Their expressions are lost in morning light;
the song of sobbing is loud in the field.

3

The song of sobbing is loud in the field
when Jonathan falls in battle
beside his father. Blood bathes
the spring barley.
We plant
The viscera of philistines
with the summer wheat. And
I am still a dead man's bondman.
Should I mourn him?
Can property weep?
Instead, I dream
Of jubilee.
To stand in my father's field again;
To be no man's golden grain,
to be no king's enslaved chaff

Yehuda

"That land there," he points,
"That was Jesse's."
We look and I consider
the bramble imprisoned by razor wire
and the story:
a day of hard words over cotton prices
followed by
a night filled with the sound of slaughtered pigs
and my great grandfather fleeing for his life to the big
    city
My Jewish family would call this a pogrom;
my Black one—just business as usual—
Black folk having their land stolen.
"They say that we could get that land back," my elder
    says.
The words hang in the air, an unanswered question
In my mother's family tree
Jesse follows Jesse with ne'er a David in sight.
I'll tell you when the Messiah has come.
When Jesse's David pastures his horse again
in that field
over there.

I recorded these words from a second cousin as he explained how my maternal grandfather ended up in Houston and how the family lost his portion of the family ranch land. It was only after I began the poem that I made the connection to King David, the son of Jesse. There is still no David, son of Jesse in that genealogical line. Note: a pogrom is a violent riot aimed at massacre or persecution of an ethnic or religious group

Scapegoats

Gen 8:20 Then Noah built an altar to the Lord and, taking of every clean animal...he offered burnt offerings on the altar.

We never saw the rainbow.
We saw Noah,
his sons, his wife, his daughters,
and then the knife.
Our saviors sacrificed us in thanks
as they prepared
to people the land
now miraculously dry.

Musings

For My Father

Three in the morn. The soul's midnight...More people in hospitals die at 3 a.m. than at any other time. —Ray Bradbury

A lonely library carrel
And your words come to me
"You read so much, you should write something."

But on such shifting soil...
the groundwork escapes me
slipping away from creosote pilings and
spilling into wetlands of grief.

I watch tiny bricks of names blur through the
microfiche reader and
There you are
One-year-old in 1920.
So I guess that the census taker came early,
before your birthday.
Your father a laborer,
Your mother a laborer,
Your fourteen-year-old brother, your six-year-old sister,
laborers
and I wonder at the hand that scribbled this label
all the way down a page that included
six-year old children and
seventy-year-old men, but
left your profession blank at one.
As if he knew
you would not remain—
and would not build your family
using the tools close at hand.

Sixty-five years later and halfway
between two censuses you died.
The long expected call coming in at three a.m.
And I, the constant reader
remember Bradbury describing that hour.
I turn over and cry myself to sleep
for the next year at least
until the second anniversary Kaddish
would find me dry-eyed
but angry
that I knew that prayer by heart
years earlier than any of my friends.
You left,
instructing me to
build my own foundation.
Washed up on this gravel-filled
beach between rotting pilings,
miles away from where your tide went out.

A Kaddish is a closing prayer of praise said at the end of each section of a Jewish service. At the end of the entire service, there is a final Kaddish said in memory of the mourner's dead. This poem was written after one of my bursts of genealogical research. My father was born in 1918 and the 1920 census is the first one in which he appears. His father was still a sharecropper at the time. It amazed me to see even his six-year-old sister listed as a laborer.

My Mother in the Mirror

There you are
again,
reflected before me
in the gym mirrors.

And I have just enough
Zen and physics,
Biology and Shinto,
To not
greet your image
with amazement.

What is time anyway?

But a cruel window
silvered on one side
And tossing back memory
like light
from twenty years earlier.

If I push this treadmill
from three miles per hour to six
Will I be running toward you?

Or away from you?

And what will that mean?

Away from slim silver pills for seizures
Away from tiny pink pills for pressure
Away from daily shots of insulin for diabetes

But also,
Away from being the first and only woman in my field
Away from a community that knows my name
Away from strangers that point me out with grudging
respect.

And what am I racing toward?

My feet
pounding,
My lungs
burning,

Pursuing
the glimmer
of my own identity
In the glare
of your
overwhelming
memory.

I once saw a photo of my mother as a young woman in her first job as a pharmacist. I was startled to see that I look like her. Like most daughters, I have been running away and running toward my mother since adolescence.

Eclipse

When I was a child,
Artemis was a slim-hipped maid.
She got one page only
in a primer of Greek myths.
One picture
one column inch,
Her shield,
a slip of silver
angled against a creamy marble pool
A smile of ivory,
her bow was carelessly tossed on night hued grass.

At seven, I was my father's goddess.
I made a Grecian robe with safety pins and yellowed
    sheets.
At midnight, rose to practice my archery.
Built a bow with limbs torn from our ancient pecan
    tree.
At midday, I defended my sister from boys twice our
    size.
Set snares for urban rabbits, if any could be found.
Taught myself to weave,
prepared myself to accept the obeisance of teachers,
And deference of distant relatives.

When I was eight, Apollo was born.

The Negro Travelers Green Book

I want to remember the things you never taught me.
Your silence made me
Listen
I saw
my cousin weeping because her lover was another's
I heard
my playmate was adopted before the word was mur-
mured in his presence.
I saw
where the family gun was hidden and I found the bul-
lets in your top drawer.

I remember all this and I have forgotten everything

I did not see
the police commissioner mount your church steps on
his horse
as people met to mourn four little girls.
I did not hear
the sounds of hammers at the state fair
loud, because we could only attend on the first or last
day
I do not know
how we safely drove from Shreveport to Houston
every summer
when there are no haven cities or colored gas stations
anywhere along our route.

The Negro Motorist Green Book was issued between 1936 and 1966 by Victor Hugo Green. It listed the private homes, the rare motels, service stations, and restaurants that would serve Negro patrons in North America.

A Singular Dying

"Whoever you are—I have always depended on the kindness of
strangers"—Tennessee Williams

With my hands encased
in these thick rubber gloves
I cannot pluck my guilt
away from my grief
even though I can pull
the car title from between
scattered receipts.

And later pass over
a college transcript,
along with other
fossilized memories
to your stalwart sister.
While marveling at her strength,
I recognize the anesthesia of
work and three hours of sleep.

Within ten minutes,
flies arrive and enter the
eyes, mouth, and
nose.

One Thursday, there had been
a long phone message
which I never answered,
sure that I would see you Saturday.
The following Tuesday, an email
arrived "I regret to tell you...
Katrina was found dead..."

Now Saturday, I arrive
with mop,
bucket,
disinfectant,
and these gloves
deceptively bright yellow.
And no one asks me why
your call was not
returned.

After 12 hours,
the flies' eggs hatch and
maggots feed
on tissue.

Your bedroom is mine
to sort and clear;
others parse out the kitchen
while I divide
important papers for the estate
memorabilia for the family.

Here, place clothes and shoes good enough
to give away.
Everything else emptied
between my gloved fingers
into great gray bags.
Abandoned treasures and trash,
dragged to the curb without a second thought
except to wonder at so many matchbooks
and so little insulin.

Within twenty-four to thirty-six hours
beetles arrive
and feast
on dry skin.

I had already steeled
myself for the
smell of death,
but there was no smell.
Only an assortment
of cherished texts,
besotted insects
and a wide empty circle
of bare concrete,
where even the carpet
had to be removed.

After forty-eight hours,
spiders, mites, and
millipedes arrive
to feed on the bugs that are there.

I was so busy that tears
did not find me
until Saturday night
alone at home.

You were single
As I am single
Weeping,
I question my lament for you
slipping quietly
into a diabetic coma.

Am I sobbing
for your youngest sister
keeping her back stiff while
praying that Tennessee
Williams's aphorism is true?

Or am I crying
tortured tears for myself
afraid to hear
the rustling vermin
beneath my own lonely bed?

Mhenga

My eyes rise from dusty wheels to the nappy hair of a
six-year-old boy who already knows that he owns this
sidewalk. His younger sister pumps determinedly on a
pink bike behind him.
"Where do you think that you're going?"
A pause.
At 45 years old, I could give the crushing reply (It's
none of your business!),
the philosophical answer (my life history),
or the guarded response of a home owner (Why are you
asking?).
"Bus Stop." I reply.
He nods, whirrs by, satisfied.
Who owns whom? I wonder.
Who tied this knot?
Who made me responsible for you
and you for me?

Swimming Lessons

Our legs scissor waves
that crash against the opposite side.
We are new swimmers
and our teachers with severe patience
lead us into the cool encompassing waters.
Their bubbling voices
are lit with funereal tones;
With fear, we watch the sunlight careen across the pool.
The glare of a summer afternoon refracts into the deep
    with sudden fire.
Some gaze longingly back to the three foot depth.
When young limbs tired there,
how natural to stand and gracefully stroll the rest of the
    way.
We were children—
We found it far simpler to walk across water
than crawl along the glistening waves.
Many of us drown
five feet away from our goal
our legs thrashing protests,
our throats throttling screams.
Each time, with soft laughter, they revive us
and send us forth again.
By the end of the week
we find an answer for terror or perish.
One boy whirrs across the length of the pool
Anxious for safety and the solid feel of the graveled
    path.
Three others consent to jump in
and out
of the fiery cauldron

never swimming again.
It is enough to brave the horror
of water enveloping the head.
Doris sulks,
Crying in the corner of the fenced area
Every day the teachers drag her over the cutting stones.
Her feet tearing and bleeding in protest,
She still refuses to enter.
Every day they rinse the thin trickle of blood
Into the dusky-blue maw of the pool.
And every day,
A cold thrill rolls through us.

You Leave

You leave,
but the place that you called home
continues without you.
You are not forgetful.
It was larger when you lived there.
The house becomes arthritic,
its bones as porous as an old woman.
The fireplace mortar is carted away by
ants.
The sand that made it
friable props up others' walls.

You leave
and your house shakes
you off like a bad dream.
It acquires children,
stylish pewter siding,
a satellite dish.
The office that your father built
but never used
is filled with books.
The double next door burns
and suddenly your double shotgun
is leader of a pack
of empty shells.

You leave
and a spring tornado takes
the flowering oak at the end of the street and
every
woman

who once lived there.
When you drive past to seek old memories
sharp male eyes measure
your possibilities.

No One Speaks

No on speaks Etruscan, a language lost
to history, all that remains are loan
words and a few brilliant images.
I hover a hand above a museum wall.
I could slip into one of these
reproductions. I'll stand
behind the young man who plays
a double flute between fern-like trees.
I'll join the dancing
matron, her arm raised in an artful arch
while her skirts swirl around a shapely ankle
lifted high. I am
already on so many walls, my head thrown back in
unexplained laughter.
On some future earth no one speaks English.
Our rants and fears are lost to antiquity,
and curious cephalopods touch our image

Female Sexual Response

Yes, dear friend—I can
smile
and chat about this year's
soft winter;
But only if you
stay
downwind.
You see,
the spring breezes are full of your fresh
scent;
And there's only so much
a woman in heat can
stand.

A Trip to the Zoo

A creature of less than
one million years of evolution,
I am not practiced
at constancy.
And if loyalty is needed
Lover,
Drag yourself into
the she-wolf's den.
Disguise yourself as one of her cubs
and dream of that mother's devoted attention.

I am no African termite
and thus will not
construct concrete bunkers
at your side,
sealing them against your brothers.

Seeing as I am not proficient
at fidelity
I will part with you
near the swans
Slim
White
Faithful unto death;
They being absent of
my primate curiosity and
persistence in
Changing
my mind.

Evidence of Spring

1

My broom remembers it once was grass. It dreams—
hearing the sound of the scythe that tore it from
its mother. It drags
across my hard clay floors with brittle sighs.

2

Your carpet smells of sheep, of donated wool.
The living room is full of their sweat, their fear,
the echoes of their relieved bleats as they realize it is
their
hair and not their hide that the shepherd desires.

3

Ignoring my age, the earth seeks to pollinate me. My
lover
wreathes my head in chains: golden trails of
live oak blossoms. My lashes are laced with jasmine;
my sneezes scented with dandelion; my coughs with
the balm of bay leaves.

Bashert

A two a.m. posting: I'm awake

Is anyone ever?

Awake is a big word—full of potential.
One arched foot stepping
away in sand.

I trace the angular letters
on your wall and wonder
if we could be a matched set.

Bashert: Yiddish word that means "destiny." It is often used in the context of one's divinely predestined spouse or soulmate. It can also be used to express the seeming destiny of an auspicious or important event, friendship, or happening.

Not A Love Poem

This page wants giddiness
Instead
I dangle my toes into
the burble of salt water
My perch, a dock
on some imaginary shore
I have never ridden a
porpoise
in these waters
but have slammed my door
on many a shark.
Love poems are written
in black and white,
their authors not knowing
the glory of gray.

Diary Entry of a Time Traveler

I will explain
because I want you to understand
who we were.

I was in class when the towers came down.
I came out at our fifteen minute break.
I saw the news,
glanced puzzled out of the office window
because New Orleans also had a WTC
and then I went back to class.
So did the teacher.
They locked the building to outsiders
but the class went on.

On the days when New Orleans was drowning
I went to the library in Shreveport
to read the news.
I competed for PCs; I viewed internet news sites;
the unemployed looked for jobs.
Some of them murmured their
consternation. Some of them tapped their foot
as I sought pictures of my neighborhood.

Listen, I heard that there were people shopping
for groceries in Paris steps away
from where shots rang out.
Perhaps some monsieur ran out for bread,
only to find that he needed it later when
friends stopped by to console him on the death of his wife.
It's common to talk about Nero fiddling
while Rome burned. Actually, he was out of town

that day. He returned to rebuild the Palatine.
I sit on the ruins that cover his buildings and remember.
Sometimes,
I am the weeping peasant sifting
the ashes for my parents bones. Sometimes,
I am the merchant making
a fortune on concrete that year.
Sometimes,
I am the woman selling tinder
to the man with the torch, saying
Burn it. Burn it all.

Tractate Baba Bathra

I am studying Talmud
and privacy.
Discussions fly around the oak table—
windows: how wide.
Courtyard walls: where divided
The windows of this classroom are narrow
But outside, I can still see
the lovers
quarreling at the busy bus stop

Occasionally, I have the pleasure of studying Talmud with a Rabbi. The poem is named for a section that includes discussions on laws affecting privacy.

Purple Hulled Peas
a memory

I spend the evening hours canning fruit. In market stalls,
I pass the purple hulled peas with nary a wistful look.

One quart of chopped cherries
One tablespoon of lemon juice, if cherries are sweet

Every summer when I was in elementary school
one bushel of peas would arrive at our inner city doorstep.
My sister and I, my cousin and my mother would set to
     work.

Six and a quarter cups of sugar.
Two pouches of liquid pectin
Boil the canning jars and lids for ten minutes after
     washing. Leave at simmer.

If I am lucky, I grab a handful of perfectly marbled pods—
purple and parchment gold. The seams fly open
like the books they take me away from. The peas
     marimba into the metal mixing bowl,
every word necessary and specific.

Boil the cherry mixture for one minute. Add the pectin.
          Boil for another minute.
Skim off the foam.

If I am not lucky, I fight the pod like a writer struggling
     with an empty page.
I open it finally to find pellets in a filmy white placenta.

Those hems and haws are
scraped into the bowl with their firmer fellows. For
flavor.

Fill each jar leaving one quarter inch header. Cap,
seal. Boil the filled jar for ten minutes

I hated those summer sessions, despite the picturesque
    imagery of camaraderie:
women shelling peas in the fading heat of a summer day.
Every pea I buy now is frozen.
Similarly, my mother's childhood yard teemed with
    turkeys. I never saw her kill one.

After 10 minutes, remove the glass jars from their bath.
If the seal is good, you will hear the cap lock with a
    rounding pop.

If I had a daughter, she would probably write poems.

<<<<>>>>

Marian is interviewed by
Kalamu ya Salaam

Kalamu ya Salaam: Why you don't trust your impulses?

Marian Moore: At times I wonder if I have this mild version of Asperger's or whatever. Like they say, "high functioning." I say things that later I realize hurt people. That is a reason not to trust my impulses.

Kalamu ya Salaam: To protect others.

Marian Moore: To protect others. Yeah. I don't want to say something and realize that I've hurt someone, and that I've said the wrong thing, because at times I've done it. I trust my impulses for me, but I don't trust them for how they affect other people.

Kalamu ya Salaam: Is that why you not only write about yourself, but you also reinterpret reality? When I say reinterpret I'm referring specifically to the Bible. It's not so much just your interpretation—you present it not as, "I believe such and such was happening." You present it as, "Look, this was what was really happening."

Marian Moore: Well, one of the things that I found intriguing about Judaism and about Midrash in particular is that the idea was always that you would reinterpret the law for what is going on now. That is still done, there are still stories being built, but I want it to be part of that conversation to say, "This is my interpretation. This is how bringing it out of the 'thee' and 'thou' and whatever into how normal people speak." I doubt [the ancients] spoke like that anyway, because Aramaic and Hebrew both are very colloquial, blunt languages.

Kalamu ya Salaam: Euphemisms. But that's the class nature of it.

Marian Moore: Right. I do remember being shocked in a sense of going back and actually reading some of the prophets with commentary in hand, where this commentator is pointing out that this person who's invading is saying, "He will kill any man that's old enough to piss against a wall." I said, "They said things like that?" You look in the Bible, and yes, that is in there, but that's not the part they tell you about in church or anything. Your question is why I reinterpret? That's part of the reason, trying to be part of that conversation, trying to make it relevant.

Kalamu ya Salaam: Relevant or reverent?

Marian Moore: Not reverent, relevant. And I don't know if we ever know what people think—we know what they say, we know what they do, and we can infer what they think, but I don't know if we ever know completely what they think or why they're doing what they're doing. So I say, "This is what I think, and is there a connection with what you think?"

Kalamu ya Salaam: Your effort, then, is partially an effort to reveal the thought process?

Marian Moore: Yeah. To reveal the thought process, to turn it over, as if you were an engineer. See what's inside.

Kalamu ya Salaam: You're assuming, then, that people are motivated by their thoughts?

Marian Moore: I think people are motivated by a complex chemistry of thoughts and emotions and hormones. I don't think we are simple creatures. You know, scientists have said that there's no such thing as free will, because they can see that when I go to pick up this sheet of paper, the motion to pick it up has occurred before the thought has occurred, which is just weird to me.

Kalamu ya Salaam: Are you assuming that human beings are machines and they operate based on programs rather than something random?

Marian Moore: But even random is a mathematical calculation—a probability. It's not so much weird as weirdly wonderful. Maybe you have to put it that way.

Kalamu ya Salaam: That's a good subtitle for the book.

Marian Moore: It's just one of those things that just wows me, that you can't explain it.

Kalamu ya Salaam: There's a common saying particularly in the Black community: "There's a reason for everything."

Marian Moore: I don't know if there's a reason for everything. I don't think there's a reason for everything.

Kalamu ya Salaam: That's exactly my point.

Marian Moore: I don't think there's a reason for everything. No. Just recently, the synagogue I belong to, a Presbyterian church, and some Baptist churches were doing a program about Job. When the Rabbi's time came up, he talked about this book, *When Bad Things Happen to Good People*. One of the things the Rabbi who wrote the book says is that when comforting people who have had a death in the family, he's learned not to say things like, "There's a reason this happened. They've gone to a better place." People don't want to hear that. Instead he says, "Sometimes, there is no reason."

Kalamu ya Salaam: Probably no earthly reason.

Marian Moore: Right. No earthly reason, no reason that we can understand. He says he doesn't want to pray to a God who will take somebody away just to make you stronger. What kind of God is that? I would rather believe that there's no reason.

Kalamu ya Salaam: Are you saying it is better for some things to be random occurrences than it is for them to be the workings of a really sadistic creator?

Marian Moore: Yes. Definitely. [Harold] Kushner's idea is that he would rather have a God that is good than one that is omnipotent. There are people who disagree with him.

Kalamu ya Salaam: Because if he is omnipotent, put his ass in the dark, because he's got a lot of questions to answer.

Marian Moore: Right.

Kalamu ya Salaam: Do you believe that there are contradictory impulses, by which I mean, you do something for one reason but you also have another feeling about it?

Marian Moore: Definitely. I've had conflicted reasons, conflicted motives, or motives that may work in that they've gotten you to do something, but that don't necessarily mix well together. But you did the thing anyway.

Kalamu ya Salaam: I fully understand. And there's a reason why I'm asking. You're someone who converted—and not just simply converted, because growing up in Shreveport, you didn't grow up in a Jewish community. You didn't grow up in a really liberal community.

Marian Moore: Yeah. I didn't grow up knowing anyone Jewish. Shreveport is definitely very segregated.

Kalamu ya Salaam: The question I'm coming to: is your conversion a betrayal of your childhood, or a fulfillment of you as an adult, or both?

Marian Moore: I don't look at it as a betrayal of my childhood. I grew up United Methodist, which had a more liberal viewpoint [than some churches], and which encouraged education and reading. A lot of the books that I read, I read in church. I may not have gone to service upstairs, but I was downstairs in the library reading.

Kalamu ya Salaam: So the church had a library, so that you could go beyond the particular spot you were born in.

Marian Moore: Right. My mother was Baptist.

Kalamu ya Salaam: Boy, that's a different story.

Marian Moore: That's a different story. She tried to teach one year in our vacation Bible school, and somebody brought up evolution, and she was going on about how evolution was horrible and whatever. The minister came in and said, "We don't have a problem with evolution." That was the last time she taught in vacation Bible school.

At the same time, I have to say that my conversion came about at a rough time. The first day of the class that I was going to was the day before my father's funeral. He never knew anything about [my conversion]. My mother, I was scared to death to tell. The Rabbi said, "You have to tell your mother." Talking to her was just about impossible. I wrote her a letter. I told her, "I am afraid of losing you. I don't want to lose you." She said, "You will never lose me." When she moved here with me, she always talked about, "Are you going to church today?", instead of going to the synagogue. But no, she accepted it. That surprised me. I guess she figured I was going somewhere.

Kalamu ya Salaam: Your father was Methodist and your mother was Baptist?

Marian Moore: Yeah.

Kalamu ya Salaam: Then your childhood already predicted it—it predicted, if you will, your two-ness.

Marian Moore: I guess in some sense. The minister that I grew up with, his wife helped find me the first apartment I lived in. At least once, my sister, my brother, and me were over to their house [here in New Orleans,] just talking. He was asking my sister where she went to church. Her husband is Catholic, so she said she didn't convert to Catholicism, but she goes to [her husband's] church. I'm going to the Synagogue, and my brother doesn't go anywhere. [The minister] says, "Where did I go wrong?" He didn't go wrong. We all live ethical lives.

Kalamu ya Salaam: I will share something with you that I only recently fully recognized of my own family background. My paternal grandfather, I never saw him as a religious person, but he was a jackleg preacher, not associated with any particular church, or anything else like that. I never saw him reading the Bible. I was told that my maternal grandfather was a well-known Baptist preacher, had two churches, one in Violet, Louisiana, and one here in New Orleans that he founded. He was the founding minister of that church. He had 4 children. It was only recently that I fully thought about his 4 children.

My mother was either the oldest or second oldest. My mother was a pianist for the Sunday school and a teacher for the Sunday school at Greater Liberty Baptist Church. She married a man who seldom went to church, period, a military man. She had two sisters and a brother. The brother, Sherman, married a Catholic woman. Although he didn't fully convert to Catholicism, his children were raised Catholic. My aunt Naomi ended up being a divorcée who had married a Catholic man. My aunt Norma Lee, the youngest, was what the boys would have called a free thinker. She had one child, also with a Catholic man. I'm looking at the family, and saying that you could argue that there was a rejection of not Christianity, but of being Baptist. I don't think any of them saw it as that.

Marian Moore: How much of that is just being in a Catholic environment?

Kalamu ya Salaam: I think a lot of it is not just Catholicism, although that was dominant here in New Orleans. I think the people who came of age in the '40s and '50s were caught up in a society in immense transition. By the time the '60s hit, they were never going to be like the '50s again. The '40s and the '50s must have been a real tumultuous time period. I think the transition is reflected in the fact that of the four, two of the marriages did not last. Sherman remains married, but his children are gone as far as being Baptist. I don't think there was anything that they willed as much as what they negotiated, given the era that they lived in.

Marian Moore: Yeah. I'm pretty sure my father was brought up Baptist. When they moved to Shreveport, the middle class church was the Methodist church, so that's where he went.

Kalamu ya Salaam: How do you negotiate a transition? What it says is, you have to move. What movement do you choose to make? Whereas for earlier generations, there was no major social movement. They didn't have options and choices. You just lived your life. Going back, I was thinking about the question of betrayal and fulfillment, because that's similar for me. When I was younger, I was reared to be the next preacher, if you can imagine me standing at the pulpit reading from the Bible, order of service coming up, and my grandfather sitting behind me proudly. I'd leave it.

Marian Moore: You'd leave it, but I don't think you'd leave the spirit. You took the kernel of it. You took the teaching, and the caregiving, and all of that part of it.

Kalamu ya Salaam: The old folks say, "It's easy to change your mind, but it's hard to change your ways." I think that your goal is recognizing the inevitability of change and the conundrums of dealing with change, particularly in those profound moments.

Marian Moore: Yeah. I would say that's a lot of it, especially the second part.

Kalamu ya Salaam: The change was not the choice. The real change was how to deal with the transitions.

Marian Moore: How to deal with the change, which is always the hard part.

Kalamu ya Salaam: Yeah. That's what comes across strongly. I don't know if you were consciously or subconsciously dealing with that. Whether it was an impulse or a forethought?

Marian Moore: Those are the natural points of drama you see in the story, when people are conflicted about where do I go from here, what does this change mean to my life?

Kalamu ya Salaam: Are you saying that conflict is natural?

Marian Moore: I say conflict is natural in the literary tradition, because the books about people sitting down and watching television don't seem to sell well.

Kalamu ya Salaam: Let me deflate that one. I know you weren't writing this book to sell.

Marian Moore: No. Not to sell, but to say, these are my thoughts over the past few years. Kind of make concrete some of it.

Kalamu ya Salaam: You want to make concrete some of the contradictions?

Marian Moore: Not so much contradiction, necessarily.

Kalamu ya Salaam: I don't see contradictions as opposites or contending forces as much as I see contradictions as forks in the road, and you're walking, and you have to make a decision.

Marian Moore: Right. Okay. I can accept that.

Kalamu ya Salaam: Your reflection on choices that were made?

Marian Moore: Yes.

Kalamu ya Salaam: It's neither condemning nor approving, you're just observing.

Marian Moore: I'm just observing, but I have to admit, some of these [choices] are pretty condemning. Some of these are born of frustration or anger, so some of them probably deserve condemning.

Kalamu ya Salaam: Isn't that part of the emotional baggage that evidently occurs when one makes a choice, whether forced to make it or reluctantly making it, and it turns out that was not the best choice, or the choice turns out not in the way you wanted, expected, or hoped for?

Marian Moore: That's true. The results of the choice.

Kalamu ya Salaam: Yeah, the results, unintended consequences.

Marian Moore: Yeah, unintended consequences. Even realizing that I have not seen all of the dominoes fall, so these are just the first of the dominoes.

Kalamu ya Salaam: That's interesting that you say dominoes, that one causes the other to topple. Earlier, we started talking about how they [phenomena] might not in fact be dominoes. They just may be a wind blew that was totally unexpected, unforeseen. Dominoes implies that there's—

Marian Moore: —that there's a person who sets the dominoes up. That's true. I didn't say that I was consistent. It's hard to find a cliché.

Kalamu ya Salaam: I think that's what makes some of those poems so beguiling and even profound: you're not saying there's a spoiler to this and so forth and so on, or as the last line of "Eclipse" says: "and then Apollo was born."

Marian Moore: Yes.

Kalamu ya Salaam: That tells the whole story right there. It's certainly the beauty of that line that makes clear you have nothing to do with the change that occurs. This is completely beyond your control. It implies that it was not something you wished for, but at the same time, it was not something you deeply regretted. In other words, you didn't hold it against Apollo that he was born, but you recognized that—

Marian Moore: —things had changed.

Kalamu ya Salaam: Changed. Yeah. Which is a really generous reading because it's honest about how profoundness changes one's life. At the same time, it doesn't blame Apollo for changing because you don't see this as an act of willful malice on Apollo's part. Rather, this is within this society. Once he's born, stuff changes, things happen.

Marian Moore: Unfortunately.

Kalamu ya Salaam: Unfortunate for you.

Marian Moore: Right.

Kalamu ya Salaam: Going back to the discussion we arrived at rather early on, you would prefer to believe that God was good and things happen, than God caused this to happen.

Marian Moore: Correct. Makes for a lot saner.

Kalamu ya Salaam: What do you mean, saner? Sane implies rules and regulations. It makes it acceptable. It makes the birth of Apollo acceptable rather than regretful.

Marian Moore: Right. True.

Kalamu ya Salaam: Even though there is a tinge in the way the poem is written, you can't help but say, "Damn, why was he born? You done messed up everything."

Marian Moore: It is what it is.

Kalamu ya Salaam: Another African American saying. I think in our folk traditions there are two strings. One string strongly believes in the omniscience of God, and another string strongly believes life is good, but it's fucked up sometimes. You can find folk sayings—

Marian Moore: —for both of those. I try to go and read more of the African folk [tales], but there's such a distance…I'm coming to it as an adult instead of coming to it as a child. Unfortunately, people are just now beginning to use those folk tales in ways…How do I say this? I could use Apollo and Greek myth because those things have been worked over so many times and played with so many times and—

Kalamu ya Salaam: —written about. And you're a reader.

Marian Moore: And I'm a reader. I'm familiar with those, even twisted and turned and whatever. I haven't seen that as much with African folk tales. I'm just now coming to that, so it would be hard for me to play with Anansi and those kinds of tales.

Kalamu ya Salaam: They're not in your repertoire of memory and reflection.

Marian Moore: Right, and I wish I could but I can't. I tried going to these, but to me they're still distant. I could not write Midrash on Anansi, the way I could write Midrash on the Bible or even Greek myths, because Anasi is just not something I grew up with.

Kalamu ya Salaam: To be clear, you're saying that although some of this was around you, it was never presented in the ways that the other material [was].

Marian Moore: Oh yeah. Definitely. If anything, I know my mother definitely did not want superstition brought into the house. That was definitely frowned on. We didn't hear a lot of the stories that I heard later on as an adult.

Kalamu ya Salaam: How does an IT intellectual become a poet? What is attractive about poetry?

Marian Moore: I like playing with words. I've always liked playing with words. Poetry is short and can be finished, where stories seem to take forever to finish and forever to polish. I wish I could write more stories, to be honest with you, because I like narrative. Even though there can be narrative in poetry, I don't read very many narrative poems. I like narrative. I like characters, which has been my problem always with writing stories: I'm more interested in the characters than the plot. I have to admit that I just don't read long narrative poems. I never finished Dante's *Inferno*. A lot of narrative poems that seemed to go on and on, I never finished them. Because I don't read them, I don't try to write that type of thing. Poetry, in terms of catching an emotional pivot point, I think it excels in that, definitely. So that's why poetry.

Kalamu ya Salaam: Are you suggesting that you're more interested in the pivots than the continuity?

Marian Moore: Yeah. I would say I am. I'm more interested in that flashiness, in that moment of fear, as far as poetry is concerned.

Kalamu ya Salaam: The pivotal moments. When I try to explain that structure to some students, I say, "I'm not going to talk to you about character development. I'm going to talk to you about four stages. The first stage is your introduction and your scene setting, however brief it may be. The second stage is your conflict, however you set it up, there is some conflict. Somebody wants something, somebody doesn't, or whatever. The third stage is your crisis, the moment when things have to change, something has to happen. Whether you want it to or not, something has to happen. The fourth stage is resolution." I say, "That's the least interesting stage and it should be the briefest. The conflict and the crisis are the more interesting stages. You need the introduction to get people to care about the conflict and the crisis, but that's the stages."

What I hear you saying is the poetry allows you to eliminate all but the crisis part, which is interesting. Again, I go back to "Eclipse" because obviously it's not simply autobiographical, it's philosophical. This is the way you look at the world as a whole: no matter how things may be going, unforeseen things happen and change the world. I see that that's your interest in the poetry. The poetry allows you to pinpoint that specific thing. It doesn't even matter what happens next. You leave it up to the reader.

Marian Moore: Yeah. I like leaving things up to the reader.

Kalamu ya Salaam: Why do you like leaving things up to the reader? You don't think that you frustrate the reader by not telling them what happens?

Marian Moore: Frustration is good for the soul.

Kalamu ya Salaam: Expound on that one.

Marian Moore: If I were going to say that I'm capturing a crisis point in the poetry, then that crisis should continue after the poem is finished. If it continues and the person is saying, "But what happened next?", that continues the conversation. The conversation is kept alive.

Kalamu ya Salaam: The characters and the situation are kept alive. The reader mulls over it and wonders, "Am I at this point?"

Marian Moore: Right. "Am I at this point? What would I do at this point? Is this even a valid complaint?" If we were balancing a plate, what keeps that plate spinning? I want the plate to keep spinning in their heads.

Kalamu ya Salaam: That's a very wonderful metaphor. One of things I would suggest, going into a completely different metaphor: "Rather than a cut flower, this is a plant." A flower is rooted in the Earth and continues to grow. A cut flower is no longer rooted. It may look wonderful sitting on the table in the vase, but it's dead, or dying, if you will. It's not going to last. What you're looking for is work that's rooted in social and material reality. As you think about it, it continues with you, rather than [being] something that's merely on a mantle.

Marian Moore: Definitely. On a mantle is too easy to be put away. Rooted, you have to come out and water it every once in a while. You have to revisit. That means it's hard for me to get rid of books, because I want to come back to them occasionally, and see if they still speak to me the same way they spoke to me before.

Kalamu ya Salaam: Is this books in general or books that you value?

Marian Moore: Books that I value. There's far too many of them. Sometimes things change, and sometimes there are books that I value that I still would not encourage other people to read.

Kalamu ya Salaam: Because you recognize that the value is particular?

Marian Moore: Right. I had a friend who was in social work. She started reading the *Foundation* trilogy series. I'm thinking, you know, I enjoyed those when I was a kid. It has some great ideas about being able to predict how a society will run. [Isaac] Asimov was not big on characters. I said, "Do you really want to read this?" The idea of psychohistory is a wonderful idea but...She wasn't able to finish even the first book. There's definitely some things that I know that I cherish, and in some cases, I know I won't go back and read them again. But the idea, I cherish. There's some books that I cherish that I go back and read, or authors.

Kalamu ya Salaam: Give us one of each.

Marian Moore: Oh goodness, one of each. Like I say, I like Asimov's thinking. I like his plots. I like some of his works, but then, I don't think he was that good of a writer as far as how we think of writing now.

Kalamu ya Salaam: Which is what?

Marian Moore: That characterization and that human beings should be full and complete. I can't think of more than one or two women in any of his plots because he came up in the '30s and the '40s. He's very white, middle class. He's a very standard writer for that time.

Kalamu ya Salaam: For that time or that ideology?

Marian Moore: For that time and ideology. It wouldn't have occurred to him to look beyond.

Kalamu ya Salaam: Understand what I'm saying. That's a reflection of the ideology rather than of the time, because there were [other] people.

Marian Moore: Yeah. There were other people. I go back to Ursula Le Guin.

Kalamu ya Salaam: She's almost a contemporary.

Marian Moore: She's more '50s and '60s, I think. Yeah. She's 80-something now, I think. One of the stories I even gave you to read, was one that still comes back to me now. I remember reading something on Facebook where they were talking about why a lot of poor whites want to vote for Trump because they don't want to be the person who's at the bottom of the ladder. It just keep taking me back to that story that I gave you to read of hers, "The Ones Who Walk Away from Omelas," because the story is about a society that looks perfect, but the reason it's perfect is because there's a child in a basement somewhere being tortured and everybody gets taken to see that child and knows that the child is there. They accept the fact that there's one person in the society who is made to feel pain so that they can feel pleasure. She ends the story by saying, "There's always a few people who walk away from the town altogether." That story still gets me. Am I the person that stays in the town?

Kalamu ya Salaam: Obviously [you're] the person who walked away.

Marian Moore: But walks away to what?

Kalamu ya Salaam: In some cases, it's not walking away to anything, walking away from something, saying, "No. I will not accept this."
    [Your] being a computer scientist who's into poetry implies to me that you don't see the human experience as monolithic. In the sense that one thing shapes the whole human being. For you, the human experience is dialectical rather than essentialist.

Marian Moore: Yes. I would say so. Definitely. I don't see how we could be formed of one [thing].

Kalamu ya Salaam: Going back to the brief discussion we just had about Asimov, you were saying that he came up in a time period and so forth, and I said, "Yeah, but there were other people."

Marian Moore: Yeah. There were other people and there were fractions even within the science fiction community, even then.

Kalamu ya Salaam: They may not have been dominant.

Marian Moore: No. They weren't dominant. They [white men] were definitely still the gatekeepers about who got published and who didn't get published.

Kalamu ya Salaam: So that's what you were looking at? The gatekeeper function and how there was [the question of] what is considered human and who is considered human? It is oxymoronic to talk about that using examples of science fiction writers. But even the science fiction writers, they're basically talking about, what is the human experience?

Marian Moore: Yes. There are few people that tried to write about inhuman experiences. Humans tend to want to read things about themselves.

Kalamu ya Salaam: That's interesting, because when I was in seventh grade they had these little book clubs. I was reading a lot of what I would now call social biology. These were books about different animals. They followed the life cycle of a given animal. I remember Lobo the Wolf and there was a couple of other things, a fox, a wolverine, a whale. I guess you would say even though they were talking about animals, they were ending up writing as if these animals had human emotions. Lobo the Wolf was a loner and so on. I say that because recently I wrote something and I was questioning whether an elephant, which is an animal and obviously intelligent, has a self-conception of itself as an elephant. Of course, we'll never know because we don't have the language to have that discussion with an elephant.

Marian Moore: Right. Elephants are among those creatures that people have said can recognize themselves in a mirror, where a lot of creatures think that there's somebody behind the glass or something. Elephants and dolphins are among those that can recognize "this is me" in a mirror. So there's self-awareness there.

Kalamu ya Salaam: Yes. So the question is, what really makes us human? Is "human" descriptively distinctive from other animal forms?

Marian Moore: There are a lot of people who want to say human is something very different. I don't know that I [do].

Kalamu ya Salaam: There's an arc.

Marian Moore: There's an arc.

Kalamu ya Salaam: We exist at some point—
Marian Moore: —on that arc.

Kalamu ya Salaam: Rather than, "There's an arc there, there's an arc over there. We're on the other arc."

Marian Moore: "We're on a completely different arc." No, I think we're on an arc with a lot of other creatures. Who's to say that in some areas they may [not] be further along than we are. That is definitely one of the themes in science fiction: what defines humanity? Some of the [topics] are just "oh, wow" things.

Kalamu ya Salaam: Something to think about.

Marian Moore: Yeah. Something to think about, or, "Space is so vast, and space is so different." It's an awe. Some of it is just the feeling of awe. Some of it is, "If we change this, how will this change?" Some of it is playing. "Let's play with histories, or let's play with physics, and see what happens, and how will that affect us?" There's a sense of play.

Kalamu ya Salaam: I'm just thinking out loud. Is that type of play a desire to be God-like and create another world?

Marian Moore: You could say that. You know, the people that say that God created us in his image. Of course we would want to be God-like. That feeling of wanting to create is part of it.

Kalamu ya Salaam: Thank you much.